Who is Jesus?

by Sarah Jarvis

This little book is a collection of quotations in which peope describe what Jesus means to them.

First published 2010

Copyright © 2010
Autumn House Publishing (Europe) Ltd.

All rights reserved. No part of this publication may be reproduced in any form without prior permission from the publisher.

British Library Cataloguing in Publication Data.
A catalogue record for this book is available from the British Library.
ISBN 978-1-906381-62-2
Published by Autumn House, Grantham, Lincolnshire.
Designed by Abigail Murphy
Printed in Thailand.

Unless otherwise indicated, Bible verses have been taken from the *New International Version* of the Bible.
Other versions used, indicated by initials:
The Message (NavPress) = MGE
New Living Translation (Tyndale) = NLT

The One altogether lovely

I believe there is nothing lovelier, deeper, more sympathetic and more perfect than the Saviour; I say to myself with jealous love that not only is there no one else like Him, but that there could be no one. . . . There is in the world only one figure of absolute beauty: Christ.

Fyodor Dostoevsky

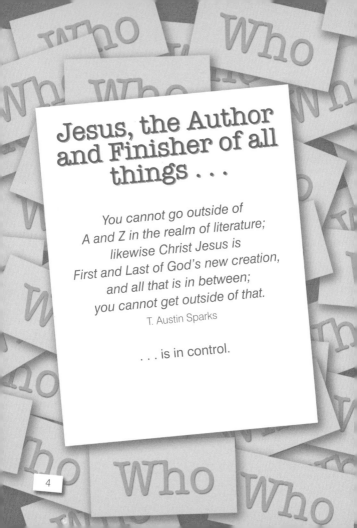

Jesus, the Author and Finisher of all things . . .

*You cannot go outside of
A and Z in the realm of literature;
likewise Christ Jesus is
First and Last of God's new creation,
and all that is in between;
you cannot get outside of that.*
T. Austin Sparks

. . . is in control.

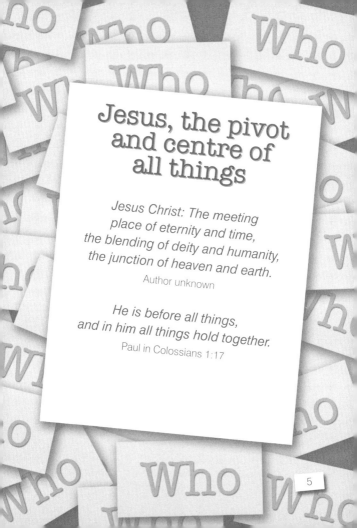

Jesus, the pivot and centre of all things

Jesus Christ: The meeting place of eternity and time, the blending of deity and humanity, the junction of heaven and earth.
Author unknown

He is before all things, and in him all things hold together.
Paul in Colossians 1:17

Because Heaven came down to Earth . . .

Jesus Christ, the condescension of divinity, and the exaltation of humanity.
Phillips Brooks

. . . Earth is lifted up to Heaven.

Jesus invites us to come to him . . .

Jesus is the God whom we can approach without pride and before whom we can humble ourselves without despair.
Blaise Pascal

. . . and promises he will turn no one away.

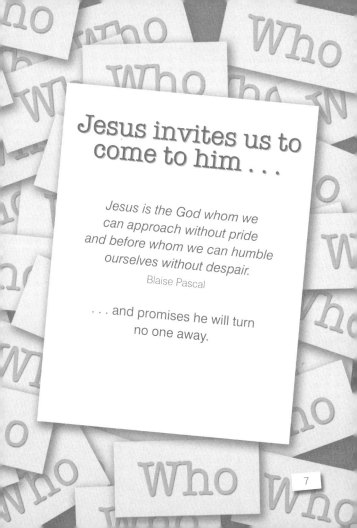

'He who has seen me...'

*As the print of the seal on the wax
is the express image of the seal itself,
so Christ is the express image
– the perfect representation of God.*

St Ambrose

*This Son perfectly mirrors God, and is
stamped with God's nature.*

Paul in Hebrews 1:3, MGE

Jesus, our only hope

*None other Lamb,
none other Name,
None other hope in heaven
or earth or sea,
None other hiding-place
from guilt and shame,
None beside Thee.*

Christina Rossetti

No Jesus, no hope.

Jesus, the only means of salvation

*Salvation is found in no one else,
for there is no other name under heaven
given to men by which we must be saved.*
Peter in Acts 4:12

*Believe in the Lord Jesus,
and you will be saved . . .*
Paul and Silas to the Philippian jailor in Acts 16:31

Christ, the bridge between God and man

In Christ Jesus heaven meets earth and earth ascends to heaven.
Henry Law

Only through Christ can God and man be reconciled.

The God-man

*Our blessed Lord combined in one,
  two natures, both complete;
A perfect manhood all sublime,
  in Godhead all replete.
As man He entered Cana's feast,
  a humble guest to dine;
As God He moved the water there,
  and changed it into wine. . . .*

*As man He climbed the mountain's height,
a suppliant to be;
As God He left the place of prayer
and walked upon the sea.
As man He wept in heartfelt grief,
beside a loved one's grave;
As God He burst the bands of death,
Almighty still to save. . . .*

*As man He lay within a boat
o'erpowered by needful sleep;
As God He rose, rebuked the wind
and stilled the angry deep.
Such was our Lord in life on earth,
in dual nature one;
The woman's seed in very truth
and God's eternal Son.*

W. A. Criswell

The Reconciler

*God was in Christ,
reconciling the world to himself, . . .*
Paul in 2 Corinthians 5:19, NLT

*Jesus was God and man in one person,
that God and man might be
happy together again.*
George Whitefield

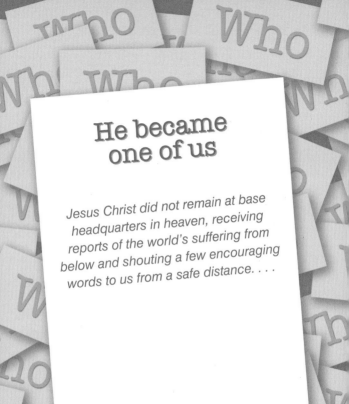

He became one of us

Jesus Christ did not remain at base headquarters in heaven, receiving reports of the world's suffering from below and shouting a few encouraging words to us from a safe distance. . . .

> No, he left the headquarters and came down to us in the front-line trenches, right down to where we live . . . , where we contend with our anxieties and the feeling of emptiness and futility, where we sin and suffer guilt, and where we must finally die. There is nothing that he did not endure with us.
>
> Helmut Thielicke

True God and true man

*If Jesus Christ is not true God, how could he **help** us? If he is not true man, how could he help **us**?*
Dietrich Bonhoeffer

Because he *is* both, he can *do* both.

The secret of a meaningful life?

Life is filled with meaning as soon as Jesus Christ enters into it.
Stephen Neill

No Christ, no meaning.

Nothing else matters

*Jesus alone **is**; the rest **is not**.*
Thérèse of Lisieux

I consider everything a loss compared to the surpassing greatness of knowing Christ Jesus my Lord.
Paul in Philippians 3:8

The greatest revolutionary

Certainly, no revolution that has ever taken place in society can be compared to that which has been produced by the words of Jesus Christ.

Mark Hopkins

What revolution have his words effected in your life?

The incomparable Man

Jesus of Nazareth, without money and arms, conquered more millions than Alexander the Great, Caesar, Mohammed, and Napoleon; . . .

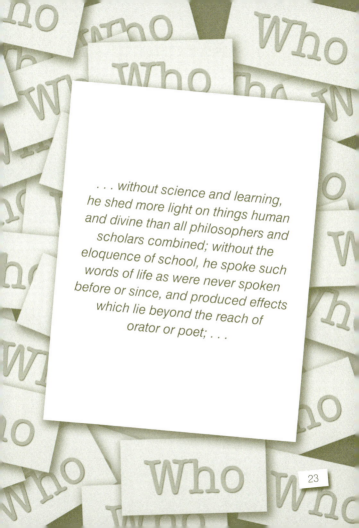

. . . without science and learning, he shed more light on things human and divine than all philosophers and scholars combined; without the eloquence of school, he spoke such words of life as were never spoken before or since, and produced effects which lie beyond the reach of orator or poet; . . .

... without writing a single line, he set more pens in motion, and furnished themes for more sermons, orations, discussions, learned volumes, works of art, and songs of praise than the whole army of great men of ancient and modern times.

Philip Schaff

His immeasurable influence

As the centuries pass, the evidence is accumulating that, measured by His effect on history, Jesus is the most influential life ever lived on this planet.
Historian Kenneth Scott Latourette

And he will be the One to bring history to a close.

The towering figure of history

Jesus Christ is to me the outstanding personality of all time, all history, both as Son of God and as Son of Man. Everything he ever said or did has value for us today and that is something you can say of no other man, dead or alive.

Sholem Asch

We believe that the history of the world is but the history of His influence and that the centre of the whole universe is the cross of Calvary.

Alexander Maclaren

The Master Teacher

Socrates taught for 40 years, Plato for 50, Aristotle for 40, and Jesus for only 3. Yet the influence of Christ's 3-year ministry infinitely transcends the impact left by the combined 130 years of teaching from these men who were among the greatest philosophers of all antiquity.

Author unknown

So sit at his feet and learn of him.

Jesus, the only Way

Jesus does not give recipes that show the way to God as other teachers of religion do. He is himself the way.

Karl Barth

As he is the only way, our only hope is in following him.

His astonishing and unparalleled claims

*Buddha never claimed to be God.
Moses never claimed to be Jehovah.
Mohammed never claimed to be Allah.
Yet Jesus Christ claimed to be
the true and living God. . . .*

Buddha simply said,
'I am a teacher in search of the truth.'
Jesus said, 'I am the Truth.'
Confucius said, 'I never
claimed to be holy.'
Jesus said, 'Who convicts me of sin?'
Mohammed said, 'Unless God throws his
cloak of mercy over me, I have no hope.'
Jesus said, 'Unless you believe
in me, you will die in your sins.'

Author unknown

Jesus, the suffering God

Christ took our sins and the sins of the whole world as well as the Father's wrath on his shoulders, and he has drowned them both in himself so that we are thereby reconciled to God and become completely righteous.

Martin Luther

Jesus suffered the penalty of your sin to save you.

A love that made a costly exchange

This is the mystery of the riches of divine grace for sinners, for by a wonderful exchange our sins are now not ours but Christ's, and Christ's righteousness is not Christ's, but ours.

Martin Luther

Your sin for his righteousness.

A love beyond comprehension

Behold, what manner of love is this, that Christ should be arraigned and we adorned, that the curse should be laid on His head and the crown set on ours.

Thomas Watson

But he was pierced for our transgressions, he was crushed for our iniquities; the punishment that brought us peace was upon him, and by his wounds we are healed.

Isaiah in ch. 53:5

Jesus, our Substitute

*Christ was treated as we deserve,
that we might be treated as He deserves.
He was condemned for our sins,
in which He had no share, that we might
be justified by His righteousness,
in which we had no share.
He suffered the death which
was ours, that we might receive
the life which was His.*

Ellen G. White

Unprecedented love . . .

No man ever loved like Jesus. He taught the blind to see and the dumb to speak. He died on the cross to save us. He bore our sins. And now God says, 'Because He did, I can forgive you.'

Billy Graham

. . . that bought your pardon.

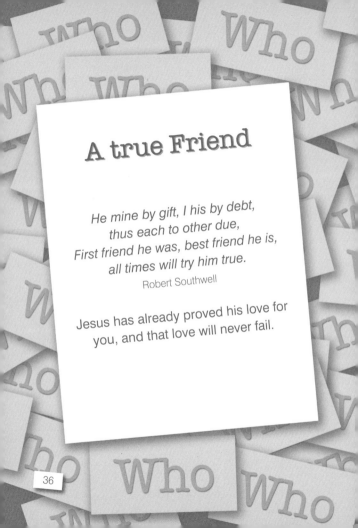

A true Friend

*He mine by gift, I his by debt,
thus each to other due,
First friend he was, best friend he is,
all times will try him true.*

Robert Southwell

Jesus has already proved his love for you, and that love will never fail.

No earthly substitute

The dearest friend on earth is a mere shadow compared to Jesus Christ.
Oswald Chambers

Jesus is the best Friend you could ever want or need.

He knows what it's like because he's been there

*In every pang that rends the heart
The Man of Sorrows has a part.*
Michael Bruce

We don't have a priest who is out of touch with our reality. He's been through weakness and testing, experienced it all – all but the sin.
Paul in Hebrews 4:15, MGE

The divine enigma

*How can we understand . . . ?
A man with human infirmities, without
human sin or sinfulness; poor,
yet having at his disposal
universal riches; weak and weary,
yet having the exhaustless
energy of God; . . .*

. . . unable to resist the violence and insults of His foes, yet able to summon legions of angels at a word or wish; suffering, yet incapable of anything but perfect bliss; dying, yet Himself having neither beginning of days or end of years?

A. T. Pierson

His is a love that defies logic.

The value of the one lost sheep

The whole Christ seeks after each sinner, and when the Lord finds it, he gives himself to that one soul as if he had but that one soul to bless. How my heart admires the concentration of all the Godhead and humanity of Christ in his search after each sheep of his flock.

Charles Haddon Spurgeon

You are very precious to him.

His unfathomable love

He loved us not because we were lovable, but because he is Love.
C. S. Lewis

A love which is unsolicited and undeserved.

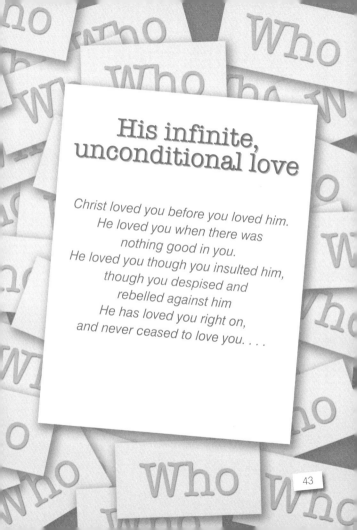

His infinite, unconditional love

*Christ loved you before you loved him.
He loved you when there was nothing good in you.
He loved you though you insulted him, though you despised and rebelled against him
He has loved you right on, and never ceased to love you. . . .*

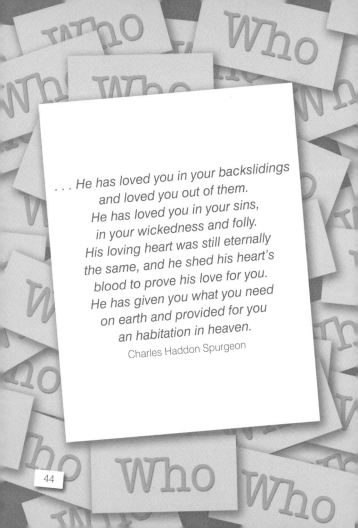

. . . He has loved you in your backslidings and loved you out of them.
He has loved you in your sins, in your wickedness and folly.
His loving heart was still eternally the same, and he shed his heart's blood to prove his love for you.
He has given you what you need on earth and provided for you an habitation in heaven.

Charles Haddon Spurgeon

Jesus' love has the power to change you

Jesus says, 'I love you just the way you are. And I love you too much to let you stay the way you are.'

Chris Lyons

If you love him, allow him to mould you into the person he knows you can be.

Love came down at Christmas

The fact of Jesus' coming is the final and unanswerable proof that God cares.

William Barclay

The incarnation was tangible proof of his love.

His all-embracing, all-conquering love

Who shall separate us from the love of Christ? Shall trouble or hardship or persecution or famine or nakedness or danger or sword? . . .
No, in all these things we are more than conquerors through him who loved us . . .

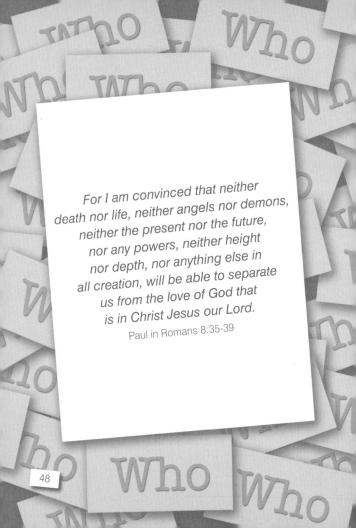

For I am convinced that neither death nor life, neither angels nor demons, neither the present nor the future, nor any powers, neither height nor depth, nor anything else in all creation, will be able to separate us from the love of God that is in Christ Jesus our Lord.

Paul in Romans 8:35-39

The sinless One who became sin

Jesus became the greatest liar, perjurer, thief, adulterer and murderer that mankind has ever known – not because he committed these sins but because he was actually made sin for us.
Martin Luther

God put the wrong on him who never did anything wrong, so we could be put right with God.
Paul in 2 Corinthians 5:21, MGE

The wonder of his atoning sacrifice

Thus, while His death my sin displays
In all its blackest hue,
Such is the mystery of grace,
It seals my pardon too.

John Newton

Now that we are set right with God by means of this sacrificial death, the consummate blood sacrifice, there is no longer a question of being at odds with God in any way.

Paul in Romans 5:9, MGE

The divine antitheses?

Christ uncrowned himself to crown us, and put off his robes to put on our rags, and came down from heaven to keep us out of hell. He fasted forty days that he might feast us to all eternity; he came from heaven to earth that he might send us from earth to heaven.

W. Dyer

He gave up everything for you, taking everything that was yours so that you could have everything that is his.

His selflessness

*Even Christ pleased not Himself.
He was utterly consumed in the zeal
of His Father's house. As man
He ever moved for God.
As God He ever moved for man.*

Geoffrey T. Bull

Jesus never thought of his own comfort.
He thought only of his Father's will
and of your future.

His humility

He had equal status with God but didn't think so much of himself that he had to cling to the advantages of that status no matter what. Not at all. When the time came, he set aside the privileges of deity and took on the status of a slave, became human! . . .

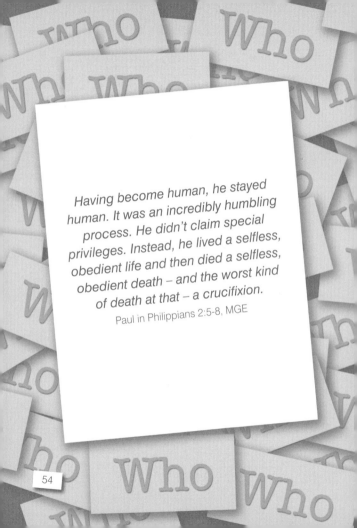

Having become human, he stayed human. It was an incredibly humbling process. He didn't claim special privileges. Instead, he lived a selfless, obedient life and then died a selfless, obedient death – and the worst kind of death at that – a crucifixion.

Paul in Philippians 2:5-8, MGE

His amazing grace

For you know the grace of our Lord Jesus Christ, that though he was rich, yet for your sakes he became poor, so that you through his poverty might become rich.

Paul in 2 Corinthians 8:9

You, who deserve nothing, have everything because of what he did for you.

He is the door

Christ's blood is heaven's key.
Thomas Brooks

His death bought your entrance into Heaven.

Jesus, the Word, revealed through the Word

No one can read the Gospels without feeling the actual presence of Jesus. His personality pulsates in every word. No myth is filled with such life.

Albert Einstein

All that I am I owe to Jesus Christ, revealed to me in His divine Book.

David Livingstone

Search the Scriptures . . .

The Bible is the cradle wherein Christ is laid.
Martin Luther

If you would know Jesus,
then read his Word.

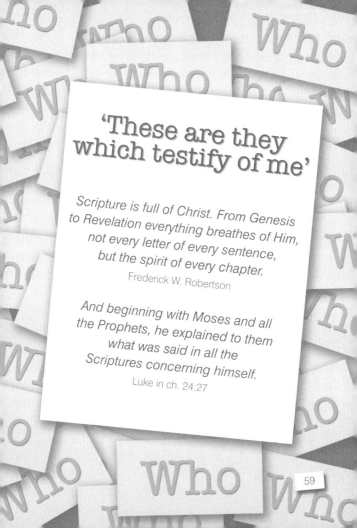

The power of his name

To holy people the very name of Jesus is a name to feed upon, a name to transport. His name can raise the dead and transfigure and beautify the living.

John Henry Newman

The name of Jesus is the one lever that lifts the world.

Author unknown

His name a source of comfort

The name of Jesus is as ointment poured forth; It nourishes, and illumines, and stills the anguish of the soul.

Angelus Silesius

And Isaiah called him 'the Prince of Peace'.

His name a healing balm

*How sweet the name of Jesus sounds
In a believer's ear;
It soothes his sorrows, heals his wounds,
And drives away his fear.*

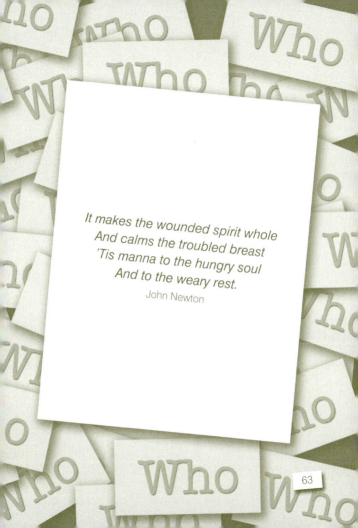

It makes the wounded spirit whole
And calms the troubled breast
'Tis manna to the hungry soul
And to the weary rest.

John Newton

There's no other name . . .

I know of a world that is sunk in shame,
Where hearts oft faint and tire;
But I know of a Name, a precious Name,
That can set that world on fire: . . .

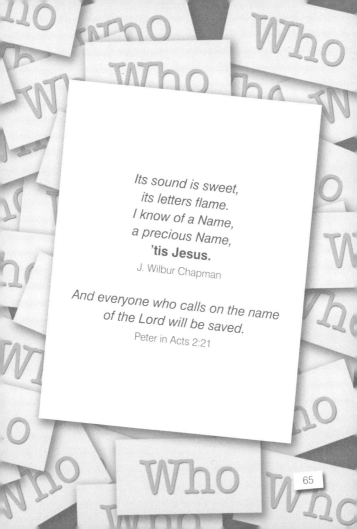

*Its sound is sweet,
its letters flame.
I know of a Name,
a precious Name,*
'tis Jesus.

J. Wilbur Chapman

And everyone who calls on the name of the Lord will be saved.

Peter in Acts 2:21

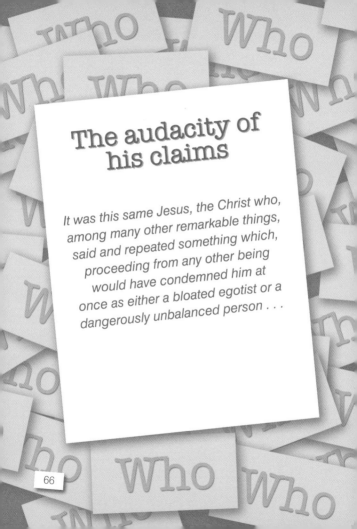

The audacity of his claims

It was this same Jesus, the Christ who, among many other remarkable things, said and repeated something which, proceeding from any other being would have condemned him at once as either a bloated egotist or a dangerously unbalanced person . . .

... when He said He himself would rise again from the dead, the third day after He was crucified, He said something that only a fool would dare say, if he expected longer the devotion of any disciples – unless He was sure He was going to rise. No founder of any world religion known to men ever dared say a thing like that!

Wilbur Smith

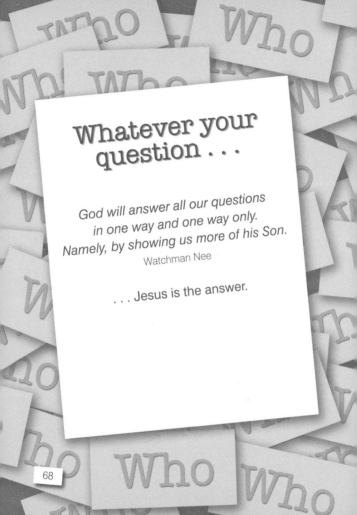

Do you have a need?

Jesus Christ is God's everything for man's total need.
Richard Halverson

Trust in Christ's ability to fulfil it.

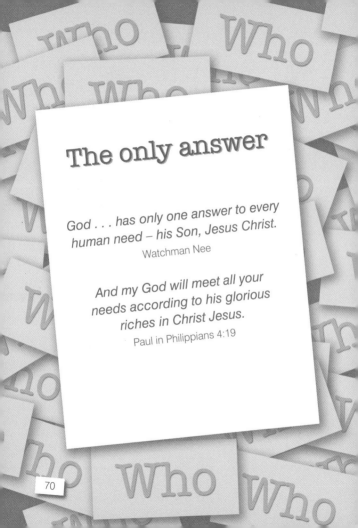

The only answer

God . . . has only one answer to every human need – his Son, Jesus Christ.

Watchman Nee

And my God will meet all your needs according to his glorious riches in Christ Jesus.

Paul in Philippians 4:19

The world needs Jesus

There is a God-shaped vacuum in the heart of every man which cannot be filled by any created thing, but only by God, the Creator, made known through Jesus.
Blaise Pascal

I have a great need for Christ;
I have a great Christ for my need.
Charles Haddon Spurgeon

All things to all men

He is a path, if any be misled;
He is a robe, if any naked be;
If any chance to hunger, he is bread;
If any be a bondman, he is free; ...

. . . If any be but weak,
how strong is he!
To dead men life he is,
to sick men health;
To blind men sight,
and to the needy wealth;
A pleasure without loss,
a treasure without stealth.

Giles Fletcher

If Christ be for us . . .

When Jesus is with us, all is well and nothing seems insurmountable. But when Jesus is absent, everything is difficult. If Jesus does not speak to us inwardly, all other comfort is meaningless. But the slightest communication from him brings consolation.

Bernard Bangley

All shall be well.

Jesus offers freedom and joy

Without Jesus Christ man must be in vice and misery; with Jesus Christ man is free from vice and misery; in Him is all our virtue and all our happiness. Apart from Him there is but vice, misery, darkness, death, despair.

Blaise Pascal

The choice is yours.

Our only hope

Lord, Thou art Life tho' I be dead,
Love's Fire Thou art however cold I be:
Nor heaven have I,
nor place to lay my head,
Nor home, but Thee.

Christina Rossetti

To whom else can we turn?

On Christ the solid rock I stand . . .

*All self-effort is but sinking sand.
Christ alone is the Rock of our salvation.*
Dr H. A. Ironside

. . . All other ground is sinking sand.

Jesus knows

He understands everything.
Helmut Thielicke

Whatever your problems, trials, suffering, Jesus understands and invites you to come to him to help you through it all.

An ever-present help in trouble . . .

Faint not, nor fear, his arms are near
He changeth not, and thou art dear.
John S. B. Monsell

And remember:
'Underneath are the everlasting arms.'

Can the leopard change his spots?

*Will power does not change men.
Time does not change men. Christ does.*

Henry Drummond

*If anyone is in Christ, he is a new creation;
the old has gone, the new has come!*

Paul in 2 Corinthians 5:17

Our Substitute for whom there is no substitute

Christ is a substitute for everything, but nothing is a substitute for Christ.
Dr H. A. Ironside

You may have all this world, Give me Jesus.
American spiritual

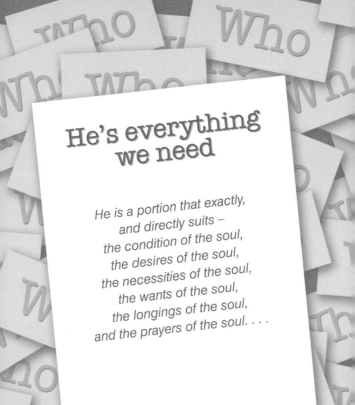

He's everything we need

He is a portion that exactly, and directly suits – the condition of the soul, the desires of the soul, the necessities of the soul, the wants of the soul, the longings of the soul, and the prayers of the soul. . . .

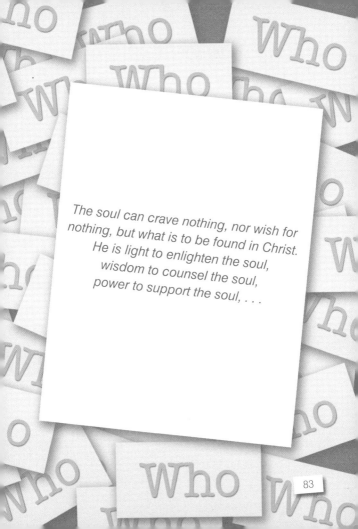

The soul can crave nothing, nor wish for nothing, but what is to be found in Christ. He is light to enlighten the soul, wisdom to counsel the soul, power to support the soul, . . .

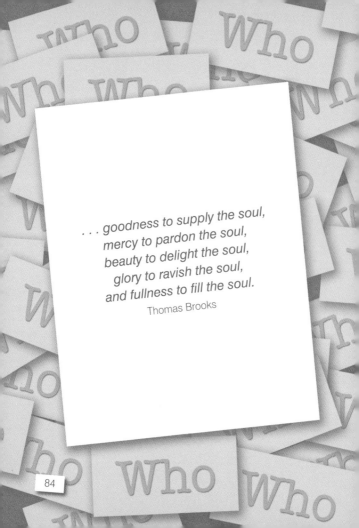

. . . goodness to supply the soul,
mercy to pardon the soul,
beauty to delight the soul,
glory to ravish the soul,
and fullness to fill the soul.

Thomas Brooks

'My peace I give you...'

No Jesus, No peace;
Know Jesus, Know peace.
Author unknown

The peace that only Jesus can offer is out of this world.

Serenity amid the conflict?

*Peace, perfect peace?
In this dark world of sin!
The blood of Jesus whispers
peace within.*

Edward Henry Bickersteth, Bishop of Exeter

Yes, but it's only possible if Jesus is in control.

The importance of his resurrection

The bodily resurrection of Jesus Christ from the dead is the crowning proof of Christianity. If the resurrection did not take place, then Christianity is a false religion. If it did take place, then Christ is God and the Christian faith is absolute truth.

Henry Morris

And if Christ has not been raised, your faith is futile; you are still in your sins.

Paul in 1 Corinthians 15:17

The promise of resurrection

He changed sunset into sunrise.
Clement of Alexandria

*For as in Adam all die,
so in Christ all will be made alive.*
Paul in 1 Corinthians 15:22

Creator and Re-creator

By a Carpenter mankind was made, and only by that Carpenter can mankind be remade.

Desiderius Erasmus

Allow him to begin the work of re-creation in you now.

His finished and unfinished work

The dying of our Lord Jesus rescues us from eternal death, whilst the doing of the Lord Jesus obtains for us eternal life.

J. M. Killen

Christ Jesus, who died – more than that, who was raised to life – is at the right hand of God and is also interceding for us.

Paul in Romans 8:34

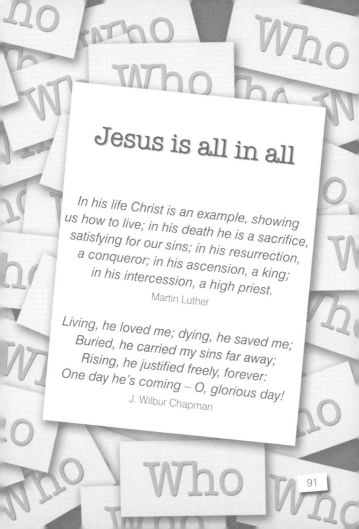

Jesus is all in all

In his life Christ is an example, showing us how to live; in his death he is a sacrifice, satisfying for our sins; in his resurrection, a conqueror; in his ascension, a king; in his intercession, a high priest.

Martin Luther

Living, he loved me; dying, he saved me;
Buried, he carried my sins far away;
Rising, he justified freely, forever:
One day he's coming – O, glorious day!

J. Wilbur Chapman

The keynote

Every character has an inward spring; let Christ be that spring. Every action has a keynote; let Christ be that note, to which your whole life is attuned.

Henry Drummond

Is Christ the driving force in *your* life?

Jesus said, 'Follow me'

No man can follow Christ and go astray.
William H. P. Faunce

And you can be sure he'll set you and keep you on the right path.

Jesus, the Light of the world

When Jesus comes, the shadows depart.
Author unknown

Only he can change your darkness to light.

Look for Jesus . . .

Look for yourself and you will find in the long run only hatred, loneliness, despair, rage, ruin and decay. But look for Christ and you will find Him, and with Him everything else thrown in.

C. S. Lewis

. . . and all you really need or desire will be yours.

A hindrance?

It may well be that the world is denied miracle after miracle and triumph after triumph because we will not bring to Christ what we have and what we are. If, just as we are, we would lay ourselves on the altar of service of Jesus Christ, there is no saying what Christ could do with us and through us. . . .

. . . We may be sorry and embarrassed that we have not more to bring – and rightly so; but that is not reason for failing or refusing to bring what we have and what we are. Little is always much in the hands of Christ.

William Barclay

No ordinary man

If I might comprehend Jesus Christ, I could not believe on Him. He would be no greater than myself. Such is my consciousness of sin and inability that I must have a superhuman Saviour.

Daniel Webster

Because Jesus is like no other, he can help you like no other.

When he has full control

When Jesus takes possession of our life, it is not only that the past is forgotten and forgiven; if that were all, we might well proceed to make the same mess of life all over again; but into life there enters this new power which enables us to be what by ourselves we could never be, and to do what by ourselves we could never do.

William Barclay

God in Jesus said it all

It is as if God the Father is saying to us: 'Since I have told you everything in My Word, Who is My Son, I have no other words that can at present say anything or reveal anything to you beyond this. . . .

. . . Fix your eyes on Him alone, for in Him I have told you all, revealed all, and in Him you will find more than you desire or ask. If you fix your eyes on Him, you will find everything, for He is My whole word and My reply, He is My whole vision and My whole revelation.

Anthony M. Coniaris

The still, small voice?

God speaks to me not through the thunder and the earthquake, nor through the ocean and the stars, but through the Son of Man, and speaks in a language adapted to my imperfect sight and hearing.
William Lyon Phelps

Make sure you're listening.

Not one jot or one tittle . . .

Never think that Jesus commanded a trifle, nor dare to trifle with anything He has commanded.
Dwight L. Moody

Jesus was serious about his Word, so we need to be serious about it, too.

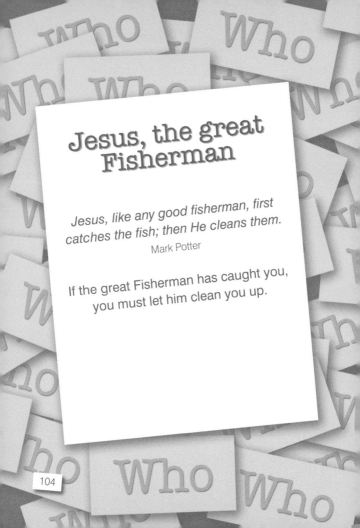

Jesus, the great Fisherman

Jesus, like any good fisherman, first catches the fish; then He cleans them.
Mark Potter

If the great Fisherman has caught you, you must let him clean you up.

Follow him . . .

What good is having someone who can walk on water if you don't follow in his footsteps?

Author unknown

. . . and he will effect miracles in your life.

The source of joy

I can say that I never knew what joy was like until I gave up pursuing happiness, or cared to live until I chose to die. For these two discoveries I am beholden to Jesus.

Malcolm Muggeridge

Let Jesus give you the joy
only he can give.

Jesus, the intrusive God?

Despite our efforts to keep him out, God intrudes. The life of Jesus is bracketed by two impossibilities: 'a virgin's womb and an empty tomb'. Jesus entered our world through a door marked, 'No Entrance' and left through a door marked 'No Exit'.

Peter Larson

He's standing at the door of your heart and knocking. Is your door marked 'No Entrance'?

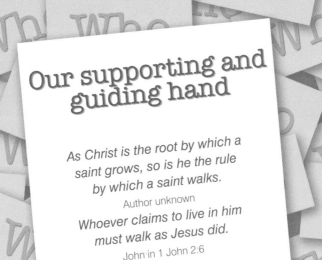

Our supporting and guiding hand

As Christ is the root by which a saint grows, so is he the rule by which a saint walks.

Author unknown

Whoever claims to live in him must walk as Jesus did.

John in 1 John 2:6

Abide in him, the Vine, and follow in his footsteps.

Nothing to fear

If I could hear Christ praying for me in the next room, I would not fear a million enemies. Yet distance makes no difference. He is praying for me.

Robert M. McCheyne

He lives forever to intercede with God on . . . [our] behalf.

Paul in Hebrews 7:25, NLT

Put him first

He values not Christ at all who does not value Christ above all.
St Augustine

If he is not Lord of all,
he is not Lord at all.

He lives and is at work

Jesus is alive and doing things!
Michael Green

Are you allowing him to do things in your life?

Without Jesus, you have nothing

Life without Jesus is like a dry garden, baking in the sun. It is foolish to want anything that conflicts with Jesus. What can the world give you without Jesus? His absence is hell; his presence, paradise. If Jesus is with you, no enemy can injure you. . . .

Whoever finds Jesus has discovered a great treasure, the best of all possible good. The loss of him is a tremendous misfortune, more than the loss of the entire world. Poverty is life without Jesus, but close friendship with him is incalculable wealth.

Bernard Bangley

With him, you have everything.

Only Jesus can give you the right perspective

Jesus Christ turns life right-side-up, and heaven outside-in.
Carl F. H. Henry

So place your life in his hands and keep your eyes heavenward.

The love he inspires...

I love to hear my Lord spoken of, and wherever I have seen the print of His shoe in the earth, there have I coveted to put mine also.

John Bunyan

Do you love him enough always to follow where he leads?

Jesus said, 'In this world you will have tribulation . . .'

The outlook is gloomy, but the uplook is glorious!
Author unknown

So keep looking up!

He is more precious than anything

Christ is a jewel more worth than a thousand worlds, as all know who have known him. Get him, and get all; miss him and miss all.

Thomas Brooks

Don't miss out. Accept him today.

The omnipresent One

As you walk through the valley of the unknown, you will find the footprints of Jesus both in front of you and beside you.

Charles Stanley

Jesus promised:
'I am with you always . . .'

His commission

*Hark! the voice of Jesus calling,
'Who will go and work today?'*
Daniel March

His authority on earth allows us to dare to go to all the nations. His authority in heaven gives us our only hope of success. And His presence with us leaves us no other choice.
John Stott

The Alpha and the Omega

Jesus Christ is the beginning, the middle, and the end of all.
Philip Schaff

Jesus Christ is the Completer of unfinished people with unfinished work in unfinished times.
Lona Fowler

He's started, so he'll finish

And I am certain that God, who began the good work within you, will continue his work until it is finally finished on the day when Christ Jesus returns.

Paul in Philippians 1:6, NLT

Allow him to complete his work in your life.

Who is Jesus?

The Shield from every dart;
The Balm for every smart;
The Sharer of each load;
Companion on the road.

The Door into the fold;
The Anchor that will hold;
The Shepherd of the sheep;
The Guardian of my sleep. . . .

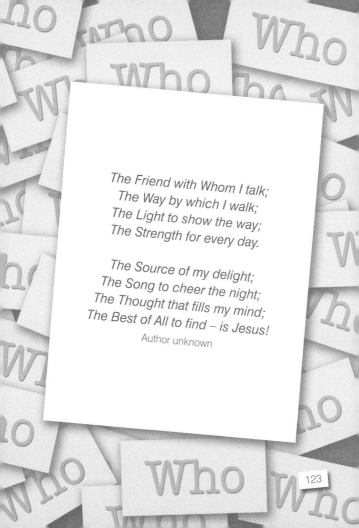

The Friend with Whom I talk;
The Way by which I walk;
The Light to show the way;
The Strength for every day.

The Source of my delight;
The Song to cheer the night;
The Thought that fills my mind;
The Best of All to find – is Jesus!

Author unknown

He was everyone, only much taller

Let us call the roll of some of the professions:
To artists,
He is the One altogether lovely.
To architects,
He is the Chief Cornerstone.
To physicians,
He is the Great Physician. . . .

To preachers,
He is the Word of God.
To philosophers,
He is the Wisdom of God.
To the dying,
He is the Resurrection and the Life.
To geologists,
He is the Rock of ages. . . .

To farmers,
He is the Lord of the harvest.
To professors,
He is the Master Teacher.
To prodigals,
He is the forgiving Father.
To the lost sheep,
He is the Good Shepherd. . . .

To thirsty souls,
He is the Water of life.
To the hungry,
He is the Bread of life.
To philanthropists,
He is God's Unspeakable Gift.

Herbert C. Gabhart

What is he to *you*?

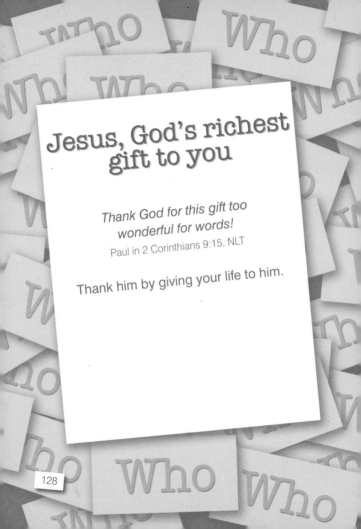

Jesus, God's richest gift to you

Thank God for this gift too wonderful for words!
Paul in 2 Corinthians 9:15, NLT

Thank him by giving your life to him.